Hawaii
The Big Island

Clinton Hood

ISBN-13:

978-1502452047

ISBN-10:

1502452049

CRATER RIM TRAIL
THURSTON LAVA TUBE 0.5
KILAUEA IKI TRAIL 0.6

www.ingramcontent.com/pod-product-compliance
Lightning Source LLC
Chambersburg PA
CBHW041510280526
45792CB00004B/1198